CONTENTS

The Clocky alarm

INTRODUCTION

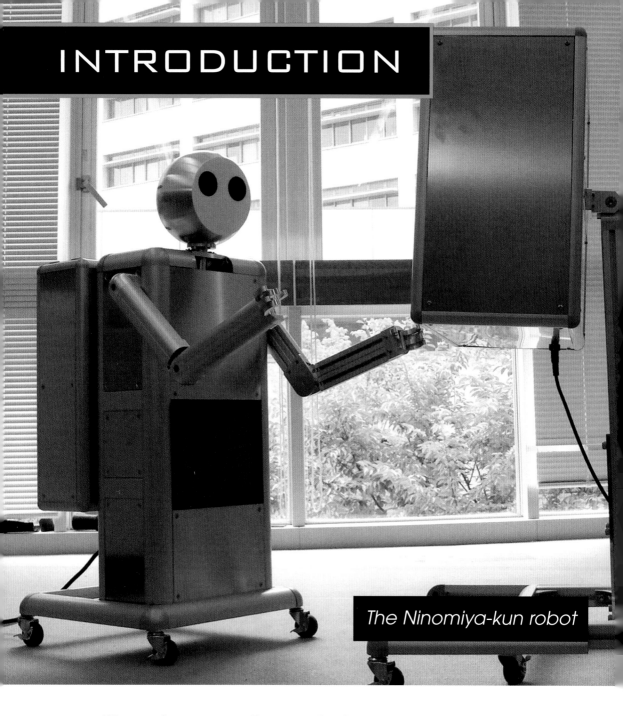

The Ninomiya-kun robot

If you've ever hoped, dreamed and wished for a cool new gadget to rock your world – look no further.

COOL STUFF

Ben Hubbard

Scarpar Powerboard

600

Publisher: Melissa Fairley
Art Director: Faith Booker
Editor: Victoria Garrard
Designer: Emma Randall
Production Controller: Ed Green
Production Manager: Suzy Kelly

ISBN: 978 1 84898 217 8

Copyright © *TickTock* Entertainment Ltd. 2010
First published in Great Britain in 2010 by *TickTock* Entertainment Ltd.,
The Old Sawmill, 103 Goods Station Road, Tunbridge Wells, Kent, TN1 2DP

Printed in China
1 3 5 7 9 10 8 6 4 2

Picture credits (t=top; b=bottom; c=centre; l=left; r=right; OFC=outside front cover; OBC=outside):
Sharon Bobrow: 19 (main). Courtesy of AbsolutelyNew, Inc.: 13t. Courtesy of Artanova: 13b. Courtesy of Gerald W.
Winkler (http://www.gekkomat.de): 18. Courtesy of Hybra Advance Technology and AbsolutelyNew, Inc.: 26 (both).
Courtesy of iHouse Tecnologia Ltda (www.ihouse.com.br): 12. Courtesy of LG: 27 (both). Courtesy of Rubato
Productions via Concerthands.com: 23. Courtesy of Scarpar Pty Ltd.: 1, 14–15 (all). Courtesy of YikeBike: 16 (all).
Fabien Cousteau: 29 (both). Michael Crabtree/Reuters/Corbis: 24–25. Firebox.com: 2, 11 (both), 21. Luis Galvez: 19bl.
Mike Hoover: 5b, 28. Nick Shotter (inventor and builder of 4MC): 17. © Nadine Meisel & Ena Macana 2005: 10.
Copyright (©), 2009 Hybrid Recognition Technologies, Ltd, All rights reserved: 4, 9. Shutterstock: OFC, 6 (dog), 22,
OBC. Sam Toren/Alamy: 8. Uncle Milton Industries: 7 (all). Used by permission of Sony Electronics Inc.: 5t, 20.
www.RoamEOforPets.com: 6 (dog collar and GPS).

Thank you to Lorraine Petersen and the members of nasen

Every effort has been made to trace copyright holders, and we apologize in advance for any omissions.
We would be pleased to insert the appropriate acknowledgements in any subsequent edition of this publication.

NOTE TO READERS
The website addresses are correct at the time of publishing. However, due to the ever-changing
nature of theinternet, websites and content may change. Some websites can contain links that
are unsuitable for children. The publisher is not responsible for changes in content or website
addresses. We advise that Internet searches be supervised by an adult.

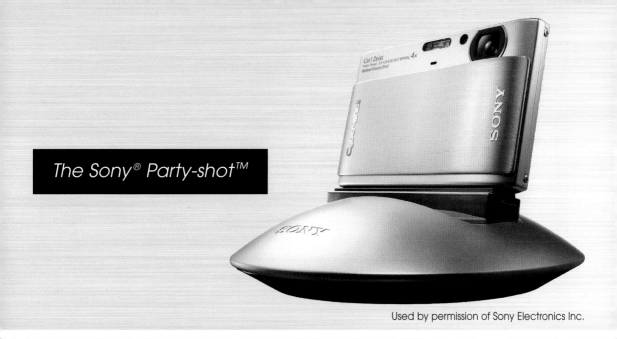

The Sony® Party-shot™

Used by permission of Sony Electronics Inc.

The Troy shark submarine

Talking robots, spinning cameras and shark submarines are no longer just daydreams.

Read on for a sensational round-up of the latest gizmos and gadgets.

Ever had a pet dog that loved running away – despite your calls, shouts and screams?

Now you can find your escaped pet with the RoamEO dog collar. A hand-held screen tracks the dog up to five kilometres away, using GPS (Global Positioning System).

RoamEO dog collar

GPS

Now your pet can snap its own photos to show you. The Pet's Eye View camera attaches to your pet's collar and can take a picture every one, ten or 15 minutes.

Pet's Eye View

Photos taken by the Eye View camera.

ROBOTS

This new robot looks and moves just like a real fish.

However, this fish has a purpose – it finds pollution around ports. The 1.5-metre long robot can detect pollution like an oil spill and transmit a warning back to base.

If you've ever wanted to keep reading but your eyelids are drooping, this robot can take over. The one-metre-high Japanese Ninomiya-kun robot reads books from a special stand using its camera eyes. It uses text-recognition software to read the words, and speaks through a voice synthesizer.

The Ninomiya-kun robot

ALARM CLOCKS

Do you have trouble getting up in the morning? These alarm clocks may be just what you need...

The Blowfly alarm escapes from its base and flies around the room, making buzzing noises. It does this until you get up, catch it and return it to its home. This alarm was made for a design project. Unfortunately it is not available to buy.

The Clocky alarm rolls off your bedside table and hides, all while its alarm beeps loudly. The only option is to get up, find it and turn it off.

AT HOME

If you like your water temperature and pressure to be perfect, but can't be bothered to keep turning the tap - this is for you!

The Smartfaucet recognizes your face and adjusts the water temperature and pressure to your personal settings. The screen also displays your email and a calendar, all while you wash.

Ever woken up in the night needing to use the toilet, but can't find the door or light switch? The illumi-knob attaches to your door handle and turns on a gentle light if it senses movement.

The Athena sofa contains a computer, a wireless connection, an ipod dock, an MP3 player and built-in loudspeakers. Inside each armrest is a flatscreen and keyboard, ready to pop out at your command.

SKATEBOARD

The Scarpar Powerboard is a motorized board that uses tracked wheels to cruise over almost any surface – from rocky ground to sand or snow.

The Scarpar Powerboard should be available to buy soon. The Powerboard will be able to reach a top speed of 60 kilometres per hour!

The YikeBike™ is a folding electric bicycle, which will be available to buy soon. It will run for about half an hour on a 30-minute charge.

- 51-cm front wheel
- Motor: 1.5 kw electric
- Weight: 10 kilograms
- Nano-lithium-phosphate battery
- 30-minute charge time
- 9–10 kilometre range
- Electronic anti-skid brakes
- Hand grips featuring indicators, lights and controls
- Top speed: 20 kilometres per hour

The YikeBike™ folds up neatly.

The 4MC is a four-wheeled motorbike.
It is much safer than two-wheeled bikes.

- Four wheels
- Motor: 125cc–400cc
- Weight: 160–200 kilograms
- Width: 58 centimetres –
  the same as a two-wheeled bike
- Features an anti-tilting device which
  means the bike can lean over at an
  incredible angle without tipping over.

GETTING UP AND DOWN

The Gekkomat turns you into a genuine wall climber, like a lizard – or Spider-Man.

The vacuum pads attach to your feet and hands and suck you tightly onto a wall using air from a tank on your back.

Rescue Reel can help you escape from the top of a high-rise building. Like a giant fishing reel, a strong Kevlar cord unravels slowly, letting you down the side of the building.

CAMERAS

The Sony® Party-shot™ device rotates, tilts and zooms the Cyber-shot™ camera. This camera then uses facial recognition to know when to take the pictures.

Cyber-shot™ camera

Carl Zeiss
Vario-Tessar 3.5-4.6/6.18-24.7 OPTICAL 4x
Optical SteadyShot

SONY

The Sony® Party-shot™ device

The Veho Muvi Micro DV Camcorder is so small, it has room for only one button – record. The 5.5-centimetre long video recorder can hang from your neck or attach to a helmet.

Actual size

The Veho Muvi Micro DV Camcorder

Would you like to jump two metres into the air or run at more than 40 kilometres per hour?

Powerbocks are spring-loaded stilts that attach to your feet. Experts say that with only 30 minutes of practice, you too can become a human kangaroo.

Practice may be the most boring part of learning to play the piano. But help is now here! The Concert Hands system guides your hands along a track in front of the keyboard. A gentle pulse in the finger gloves lets you know when to hit each key.

The Concert Hands teaching system.

THE AQUADA

The Gibbs Aquada is a high-speed vehicle that can travel both in water and on land. Just drive it into the water and you're sailing away!

- Transforms from car to boat in six seconds
- Top speed of 160 kilometres per hour on land
- Top speed of 50 kilometres per hour in water
- Jet-propulsion system
- V6 four-speed engine

PHONES

People normally connect their bluetooth devices to their mobile phones and wear them on their ears.

The ORB™ bluetooth headset can also be worn as a ring.

The ORB™ ring still displays things like caller ID and calendar information.

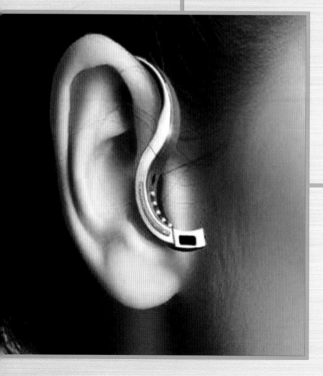

For those who want to make a call from their watch, the LG-GD910 is for you. This touch-screen watch phone has everything you could wish for, including a camera and an MP3 player.

SHARK SUBMARINE

"Troy" is a submarine built to look, move and even behave like a great white shark. It was designed to get as close as possible to the massive predator in its natural environment.

"The whole point is to fool them into thinking I'm a shark."
– Fabien Cousteau, inventor

Troy specs:
- Weight: 545 kilograms
- Length: 4.3 metres
- Plastic, rubber and elastic skin
- Three cameras
- Escape hatch in the head for a quick exit
- Silent movement
- The passenger requires a wetsuit
  and scuba-diving gear to breathe.

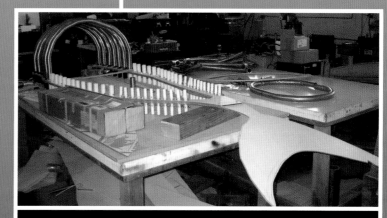

Troy has five-centimetre-thick stainless steel ribs.

bluetooth Wireless technology used for transferring information at high speed.

cc Cubic centimetre; used to measure the size of an engine.

dock A platform or base for an electronic device.

GPS (Global Positioning System) A navigation system based on information sent from satellites around the planet.

Kevlar A special man-made fibre of great strength.

lithium-ion Describes a rechargeable battery that uses the metallic element lithium; it provides twice the energy of an ordinary battery.

motorized To add a motor to something to make it go faster.

pollution Contamination of the environment due to human activities.

port A town or city built next to a harbour where ships load and unload cargo.

pulse A gentle vibration at regular intervals.

stilts Upright poles that allow the user to walk high above the ground.

synthesizer A machine that electronically produces sounds.

transmit To broadcast or send out information.

V6 A six-cylinder engine.

wetsuit A tight-fitting rubber suit that helps to keep the wearer warm in cold water.

DID YOU KNOW?

- In 1943 president of IBM Thomas Watson said he thought there was a market for only five computers worldwide.
- In 1946 movie executive Darryl Zanuck predicted television would be dead within six months of it being launched.
- In 2004 Microsoft founder Bill Gates said there would be no more spam emails by 2006.
- In 1876, the head of the British Post Office said America may need telephones but Britain did not – it had plenty of messenger boys instead.

COOL STUFF ONLINE

Here are some websites dedicated to the latest technology in gadgets and electronics:

http://www.coolest-gadgets.com

http://www.engadget.com

http://www.gadgetmadness.com

http://www.gizmoactive.com

http://gizmodo.com

http://www.wired.com

INDEX